Vintage Cushions

hachette
PARTWORKS LTD

Contents

Welcome

Bring a retro feel to your living space with these fabulous vintage cushions. There are designs with a distinctly 1930s look and others that rock a swinging 60s vibe! Pick your favourite decade and get knitting!

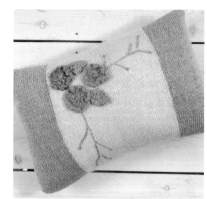

Remember to look out for the stitch library, step-by-step instructions and knitting school tutorials throughout the book.

The tenth square for your amazing throw has cables, bobbles and moss stitch - an exciting and challenging mix!

Scattered Petals

Measurements

Cushion measures 46cm square

Materials

HOW MUCH YARN:

2 x 100g balls of Patons 100%
Cotton 4 ply in main colour
A – Jade (shade 01726)

1 ball in each of four contrast
colours: B – Candy (shade 01734);
C – Lilac (shade 01701);
D – Nectarine (shade 01723) and
E – Yellow (shade 01740)

NEEDLES:

Pair of 3.25mm (no. 10) needles

ADDITIONAL ITEMS:

4 buttons

46cm square cushion pad

○ This cushion is worked in jewel-bright colours and makes a striking note on a sofa or bed.

Tension

28 sts and 36 rows measure 10cm square over st st on 3.25mm (no. 10) needles

IT IS ESSENTIAL TO WORK TO THE STATED TENSION TO ACHIEVE SUCCESS

Cushion front

With 3.25mm (no. 10) needles and A, cast on 128 sts. Beg with a k row, cont in st st until work measures 46cm from beg, ending with a p row. Cast off.

Cushion back

TOP HALF

With 3.25mm (no. 10) needles and A, cast on 128 sts. Beg with a k row, cont in st st until work measures 21.5cm from beg, ending with a p row.

Next row: (K1, p1) to end.

Next row: (P1, k1) to end.

Rep last 2 rows once more to form moss st.

Buttonhole row: (RS) Patt 18 sts, (yo, work 2tog, patt 28 sts) 3 times, yo, work 2tog, patt 18 sts.

Work 5 more rows in moss st. Cast off in patt.

BOTTOM HALF

With 3.25mm (no. 10) needles and A, cast on 128 sts. Beg with a k row, cont in st st until work measures 21.5cm from beg, ending with a p row.

Next row: (K1, p1) to end.

Next row: (P1, k1) to end.

Rep last 2 rows 4 times more to form moss st. Cast off in patt.

Flowers

PETAL FLOWER

(Make 4 with B as outer colour and centre in C; make another 4 with C as outer colour and centre in D)

With 3.25mm (no. 10) needles and outer colour, cast on 68 sts. P 1 row.

Next row: K2, (k1, sl this st back on to left needle, pass next 8 sts over top of this st and off needle, (yo) twice to make 2 sts, k slipped st again, k2) to end. 32 sts.

Next row: P1, (p2tog, p1, p1 tbl, p1) to last st, p1. 26 sts.

Change to centre colour.

Next row: (K2tog) to end. 13 sts. P 1 row.

Next row: K1, (k2tog) to end. 7 sts.

Cut off yarn, thread through rem sts, draw up tightly and sew row ends tog to form a flower.

TUFTED FLOWER small(medium) (Make 3 small flowers in C and 4 in D; make 2 medium flowers in each of C and D)

With 3.25mm (no. 10) needles and required colour, make a slip knot and place on needle.

Next row: (Cast on 5(8) sts to give 6(9) sts on needle, cast off 5(8) sts, sl rem st back on to left needle) 7 times.

Fasten off rem st. Thread yarn through all slipped sts, gather up and fasten off to form flower.

Making up

Press cushion front and backs according to directions on ball band. Using photograph of cushion as a guide, sew flowers to cushion front in a random formation. Embroider a French knot with E in centre of all flowers. With RS facing, sew cushion backs to cushion front, overlapping button band over buttonhole band in centre. Turn RS out. Sew on buttons to correspond with buttonholes.

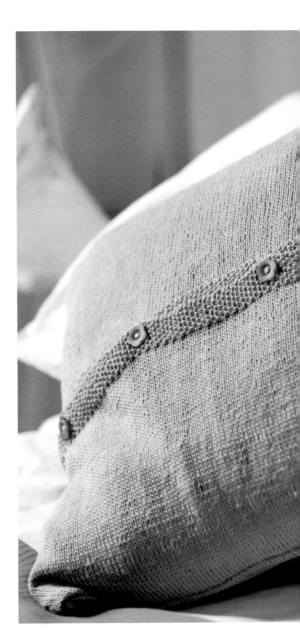

Buttoned Cushions

Choose one cushion to make or knit both in co-ordinating colours to complement your décor.

Measurements

Both cushions measure 46cm square

Materials

HOW MUCH YARN

Square pattern cover 6 x 50g balls of Sublime Baby Cashmere Merino Silk DK in Pip (shade 381)

Chevron pattern cover 7 x 50g balls of Sublime Baby Cashmere Merino Silk DK in Ruffles (shade 382)

NEEDLES

Pair of 3.75mm (no. 9) needles
Pair of 4mm (no. 8) needles

ADDITIONAL ITEMS

6 buttons for Square pattern cover
1 button for Chevron pattern cover
46cm square cushion pad

Tension

22 sts and 34 rows measure 10cm square (Square pattern) and 22 sts and 33 rows measure 10cm square (Chevron pattern) on 4mm (no. 8) needles

IT IS ESSENTIAL TO WORK TO THE STATED TENSION TO ACHIEVE SUCCESS

Square pattern cushion
Back

(Starting at lower edge.)

**With 4mm (no. 8) needles cast on 101 sts. Purl 1 row. Cont in square patt as foll:

1st row: (RS) (K1, p1) 5 times, *k9, p1, (k1, p1) 4 times, rep from * to last st, k1.

2nd row: K1, (p1, k1) 4 times, *p11, k1, (p1, k1) 3 times, rep from * to last 2 sts, p1, k1.

3rd–12th rows: Rep 1st and 2nd rows 5 times.

13th row: As 1st row.

14th row: K1, p9, *k1, (p1, k1) 4 times, p9, rep from * to last st, k1.

15th row: K11, *p1, (k1, p1) 3 times, k11, rep from * to end.

16th–25th rows: Rep 14th and 15th rows 5 times.

26th row: As 14th row.

These 26 rows form square patt.**
Rep them 5 times more, ending with a WS row and dec 1 st at each end of last row. 99 sts.
Insert a marker at each end of last row.

TOP BORDER

Change to 3.75mm (no. 9) needles. Work in moss st patt as foll:

1st row: (RS) P1, *k1, p1, rep from * to end.

2nd row: P1, *k1, p1, rep from * to end.

These 2 rows form moss st. Cont in moss st for a further 4 rows, ending with a WS row.

1st buttonhole row: (RS) Patt 3 sts, cast off next 3 sts, *patt 15 sts (including st on needle after cast-off), cast off next 3 sts, rep from * 4 times more, patt to end.

2nd buttonhole row: Patt to end, casting on 3 sts over those cast off on previous row.

Cont in moss st patt for a further 6 rows, ending with a WS row. Cast off in moss st.

Front

Work as given for Back from ** to **. Rep these 26 rows 4 times more, then 1st–13th rows again, ending with a RS row.

TOP BORDER

Change to 3.75mm (no. 9) needles. Work in moss st patt as foll:

1st row: (WS) K1, *p1, k1, rep from * to end.

2nd row: K1, *p1, k1, rep from * to end.

These 2 rows form moss st patt. Cont in moss st for a further 12 rows, ending with a RS row. Cast off in moss st (on WS).

Making up

Do not press.

With RS of Back and Front together and matching markers on Back to cast-off edge of Front, join side and lower edge seams, taking in one full st at side seams and leaving Top border of Back free. Turn to RS and sew buttons to Top border of Front to correspond with buttonholes on Top border of Back. Insert cushion pad and fasten buttons.

Chevron pattern cushion
Back

(Starting at lower edge.)

**With 4mm (no. 8) needles cast on 103 sts. Purl 1 row. Work in chevron patt as foll:

1st row: (RS) K11, *p1, k19, rep from * to last 12 sts, p1, k11.

2nd row: K1, p9, *k1, p1, k1, p17, rep from * to last 13 sts, k1, p1, k1, p9, k1.

3rd row: K9, *p1, (k1, p1) twice, k15, rep from * to last 14 sts, p1, (k1, p1) twice, k9.

4th row: K1, p7, *k1, (p1, k1) 3 times, p13, rep from * to last 15 sts, k1, (p1, k1) 3 times, p7, k1.

5th row: K7, *p1, (k1, p1) 4 times, k11, rep from * to last 16 sts, p1, (k1, p1) 4 times, k7.

6th row: K1, p5, *k1, (p1, k1) 5 times, p9, rep from * to last 17 sts, k1, (p1, k1) 5 times, p5, k1.

7th row: K5, *p1, (k1, p1) 6 times, k7, rep from * to last 18 sts, p1, (k1, p1) 6 times, k5.

8th row: K1, p3, *k1, (p1, k1) 7 times, p5, rep from * to last 19 sts, k1, (p1, k1) 7 times, p3, k1.

9th row: K3, *p1, (k1, p1) 8 times, k3, rep from * to end.

10th row: K1, *p1, k1, rep from * to end.

11th row: (K1, p1) 5 times, k3, *p1, (k1, p1) 8 times, k3, rep from * to last 10 sts, (p1, k1) 5 times.

12th row: K1, (p1, k1) 4 times, p5, *k1, (p1, k1) 7 times, p5, rep from * to last 9 sts, (k1, p1) 4 times, k1.

13th row: (K1, p1) 4 times, k7, *p1, (k1, p1) 6 times, k7, rep from * to last 8 sts, (p1, k1) 4 times.

14th row: K1, (p1, k1) 3 times, p9, *k1, (p1, k1) 5 times, p9, rep from * to last 7 sts, (k1, p1) 3 times, k1.

15th row: (K1, p1) 3 times, k11, *p1, (k1, p1) 4 times, k11, rep from * to last 6 sts, (p1, k1) 3 times.

16th row: K1, (p1, k1) twice, p13, *k1, (p1, k1) 3 times, p13, rep from * to last 5 sts, (k1, p1) twice, k1.

17th row: (K1, p1) twice, k15, *p1, (k1, p1) twice, k15, rep from * to last 4 sts, (p1, k1) twice.

18th row: K1, p1, k1, *p17, k1, p1, k1, rep from * to end.

19th row: K1, p1, *k19, p1, rep from * to last st, k1.

20th row: K1, p10, *k1, p19, rep from * to last 12 sts, k1, p10, k1.

21st row: K10, *p1, k1, p1, k17, rep from * to last 13 sts, p1, k1, p1, k10.

22nd row: K1, p8, *k1, (p1, k1) twice, p15, rep from * to last 14 sts, k1, (p1, k1) twice, p8, k1.

23rd row: K8, *p1, (k1, p1) 3 times, k13, rep from * to last 15 sts, p1, (k1, p1) 3 times, k8.

24th row: K1, p6, *k1, (p1, k1) 4 times, p11, rep from * to last 16 sts, k1, (p1, k1) 4 times, p6, k1.

25th row: K6, *p1, (k1, p1) 5 times, k9, rep from * to last 17 sts, p1, (k1, p1) 5 times, k6.

26th row: K1, p4, *k1, (p1, k1) 6 times, p7, rep from * to last 18 sts, k1, (p1, k1) 6 times, p4, k1.

27th row: K4, *p1, (k1, p1) 7 times, k5, rep from * to last 19 sts, p1, (k1, p1) 7 times, k4.

28th row: K1, p2, *k1, (p1, k1) 8 times, p3, rep from * to last 20 sts, k1, (p1, k1) 8 times, p2, k1.

29th row: K2, p1, *k1, p1, rep from * to last 2 sts, k2.

30th row: K2, (p1, k1) 4 times, p3, *k1, (p1, k1) 8 times, p3, rep from * to last 10 sts, (k1, p1) 4 times, k2.

31st row: K2, p1, (k1, p1) 3 times, k5, *p1, (k1, p1) 7 times, k5, rep from * to last 9 sts, (p1, k1) 3 times, p1, k2.

32nd row: K2, (p1, k1) 3 times, p7, *k1, (k1, p1) 6 times, p7, rep from * to last 8 sts, (p1, k1) 3 times, k2.

33rd row: K2, p1, (k1, p1) twice, k9, *p1, (k1, p1) 5 times, k9, rep from * to last 7 sts, (p1, k1) twice, p1, k2.

34th row: K2, (p1, k1) twice, p11, *k1, (p1, k1) 4 times, p11, rep from * to last 6 sts, (k1, p1) twice, k2.

35th row: K2, p1, k1, p1, k13, *p1, (k1, p1) 3 times, k13, rep from * to last 5 sts, p1, k1, p1, k2.

36th row: K2, p1, k1, p15, *k1, (p1, k1) twice, p15, rep from * to last 4 sts, k1, p1, k2.

37th row: K2, p1, k17, *p1, k1, p1, k17, rep from * to last 3 sts, p1, k2.

38th row: K2, p19, *k1, p19, rep from * to last 2 sts, k2.

These 38 rows form chevron patt. Rep them 3 times more, ending with a WS row.**

FLAP

Change to 3.75mm (no. 9) needles. Work in moss st as foll:

Next row: (RS) P1, *k1, p1, rep from * to end.

Work 1 more row in moss st as set. Insert a marker at each end of last row.

Next row: Sl 1k, k1, psso, moss st to last 2 sts, k2tog. 101 sts.

Keeping moss st correct as set throughout, work 3 rows, ending with a WS row.

SHAPE SIDES

Next row: (RS) K1, p1, sl 1k, k2tog, psso, moss st to last 5 sts, k3tog, p1, k1.

Work 3 rows.

Rep last 4 rows 21 times more, ending with a WS row. 13 sts.

Next row: K1, p1, sl 1k, k2tog, psso, cast off next 3 sts in moss st, slip st on right-hand needle after cast-off back onto left-hand needle, k3tog (including st just slipped back), p1, k1.

Next row: Moss st to end, casting on 3 sts over those cast off on previous row. 9 sts.

Work 2 rows.

Next row: (RS) K1, p1, sl 2k, k3tog, p2sso, p1, k1. 5 sts.

Next row: K1, (p1, k1) twice.

Next row: K1, p3tog, k1. 3 sts.

Next row: K1, p1, k1.

Next row: Sl 1k, k2tog, psso. Fasten off.

Front

Work as given for Back from ** to **.

TOP BORDER

Change to 3.75mm (no. 9) needles. Work in moss st as foll:

Next row: (RS) P1, *k1, p1, rep from * to end.

Next row: P1, *k1, p1, rep from * to end.

Cast off in moss st.

Making up

Do not press.

With RS of Back and Front together and matching markers on Back to cast-off edge of Front, join side and lower edge seams, taking in one full st at side seams and leaving Flap free. Turn to RS and sew button to Front to correspond with buttonhole on Flap. Insert cushion pad and fasten button.

Four-stitch Cable

Cable stitches make textured patterns. To make a cable, the stitches are worked in a different order on specific rows, so they cross over and create a rope-like pattern.

This cable pattern is created by slipping two stitches onto a separate cable needle and leaving them at the front of the work, working the next two stitches in the row, then knitting the held stitches. This takes the stitches diagonally across the front of the two stitches just knitted to give a twisted rope effect. Holding the stitches in the front of the fabric results in a cable that twists to the left; if they are held on a needle at the back of the work the cable twists to the right.

❶ Cast on the required number of stitches. On the first row, purl six stitches, then take the yarn to the back of the work and knit the next four stitches. Repeat this sequence to the last six stitches and then purl these.

② On the second row, knit the first six stitches and then purl the next four stitches. Repeat this sequence to the last six stitches and knit these. Repeat the first and second rows.

③ The fifth row sets the cable pattern. Purl the first six stitches. Slip the next two stitches onto a cable needle and leave them at the front of the fabric. Knit the next two stitches.

④ Knit the two stitches held on the cable needle in the same order that they would have appeared originally in the row. You can slip the stitches back onto the left-hand needle and knit them from this needle instead of the cable needle if you find this easier.

⑤ Repeat steps 3 and 4 to the last six stitches and then purl these. You can now see the twisted rope pattern emerging on the cable panels.

⑥ Repeat the second row to give the sixth row of the pattern. These six rows are repeated until you have the length of cable required.

HOW TO WORK THE PATTERN

This is how the instructions for this four-stitch cable would be given in a pattern:

1st and 3rd rows: (RS) *P6, k4, rep from * to last 6 sts, p6.
2nd and 4th rows: *K6, p4, rep from * to last 6 sts, k6.
5th row: *P6, C4F, rep from * to last 6 sts, p6.
6th row: As 2nd and 4th rows.

These six rows form the pattern and are repeated for the length given in the pattern. Sometimes this is given as a number of repeats of the pattern.

On Target

○ Hit the bulls-eye with this striking cushion in a great shade of indigo blue.

Measurements
Cushion measures 45 x 45cm

Materials
HOW MUCH YARN

6 x 50g balls of Debbie Bliss Rialto Aran in colour A – Indigo (shade 37)

1 ball in colour B – Cream (shade 16)

NEEDLES

Pair of 4.5mm (no. 7) needles

Pair of 5mm (no. 6) needles

ADDITIONAL ITEMS

3 x 29mm self-cover buttons

Needle and sewing thread

45cm square cushion pad

Tension
18 sts and 24 rows measure 10cm square over st st on 5mm (no. 6) needles

IT IS ESSENTIAL TO WORK TO THE STATED TENSION TO ACHIEVE SUCCESS

Note: When working from the large chart, read odd-numbered (RS) rows from right to left and even-numbered (WS) rows from left to right. Use separate balls of yarn where necessary, twisting yarns tog on WS of work when changing colour to avoid a hole forming. Do not strand yarn across WS of work.

Front

With 5mm (no. 6) needles and A, cast on 84 sts. Beg with a k row, work 14 rows in st st, ending with a WS row. Cont in patt from chart as foll:

1st row: K12 A, k across 60 sts from 1st row of chart, k12 A.

2nd row: P12 A, p across 60 sts from 2nd row of chart, p12 A.

Cont in patt from chart as set until all 80 rows have been completed, ending with a WS row. Cut off B. Cont in A only, work 14 more rows in st st, ending with a WS row. Cast off.

Back

TOP SECTION

With 5mm (no. 6) needles and A, cast on 84 sts. Beg with a k row, work 44 rows in st st, ending with a WS row.

Next row: (RS) P1, (k2, p2) to last 3 sts, k2, p1.

Next row: K1, (p2, k2) to last 3 sts, p2, k1.

Rep last 2 rows 4 times more.

1st buttonhole row: (RS) Rib 20 sts, cast off next 4 sts, (rib 16 sts including st used to cast off, cast off next 4 sts) twice, rib to end.

2nd buttonhole row: Rib to end, casting on 4 sts over those cast off in previous row.

Work 8 more rows in rib. Cast off in rib.

LOWER SECTION

Work as given for Top section, omitting buttonholes.

Button covers *(make 3)*

With 4.5mm (no. 7) needles and A, cast on 6 sts.

1st row: (RS) Inc in first st, k to last st, inc in last st. 8 sts.

2nd row: P to end.

3rd–7th rows: Join in B and work in patt from 1st–5th rows of small chart, stranding yarns across WS of work. Cut off B and cont in A only.

8th row: P to end.

9th row: K2tog, k4, k2tog. 6 sts. Cast off.

Making up

Press using a warm iron over a dry cloth and avoiding flattening ribbing. Lay cushion front RS up and place top section of back on top with RS down and matching cast-on edges. Place lower section of back in position, matching cast-off edges and overlapping ribbing in centre. Backstitch together around outer edges and turn RS out.

Work running st around outer edge of button piece, place centrally over button, gather up stitching and secure. Apply button back to hold in place. Repeat for each button. Sew on buttons to correspond with buttonholes. Insert cushion pad and button closed.

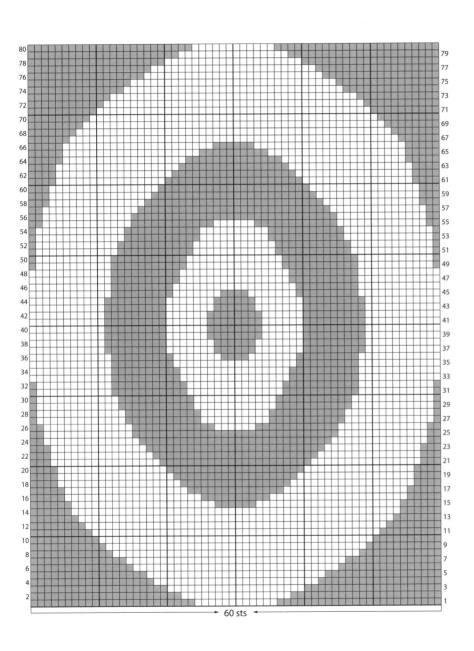

= A

= B

8 sts

Chevron Stripes

○ Colourful chevron stripes give this sleek buttoned cushion 1930s class.

Measurements

Cushion measures 40cm square

Materials

HOW MUCH YARN:

1 x 50g ball of Debbie Bliss Rialto DK in each of five colours: A – Grey (shade 04); B – Teal (shade 20); C – Apple (shade 09); D – Lavender (shade 52) and E – Aqua (shade 44)

NEEDLES:

Pair of 3.25mm (no. 10) needles
Pair of 4mm (no. 8) needles

ADDITIONAL ITEMS:

4 stitch markers
5 buttons
40cm square cushion pad

Tension

20 sts (1 patt rep) and 22 rows measure 8cm square over patt on 4mm (no. 8) needles

IT IS ESSENTIAL TO WORK TO THE STATED TENSION TO ACHIEVE SUCCESS

Cushion
(knitted in one piece, beg with top section of back)

With 3.25mm (no. 10) needes and A, cast on 101 sts. K 2 rows.

Buttonhole row: K10, (yfwd and yrn to make 2 sts, k2tog, k18) 4 times, yfwd and yrn, k2tog, k9.

Next row: K to end, dropping the extra loops at each buttonhole. 101 sts.

Change to 4mm (no. 8) needles. Cont in chevron patt as foll:

1st row: (RS) K1, (m1, k8, sl 1, k2tog, psso, k8, m1, k1) to end.

2nd row: P to end.

Rep these 2 rows to form patt. Cont in patt, working in stripes as foll:

4 rows B, 2 C, 6 D, 2 B, 4 A, 4 E, 6 B, 2 D, 4 C and 2 B.

Mark each end of last row to indicate start of front.

Cont in patt, work 2 rows more B, 4 C, 2 D, 6 B, 4 E, 4 A, 2 B, 6 D, 2 C, 4 B, 4 A, 4 D, 2 C, 2 B, 2 C, 4 A, 4 D, 6 E, 2 B, 4 D, 6 C, 4 A, 4 B, 2 E, 4 D, 4 E, 6 A, 2 D, 4 C, 2 E and 2 B.

Mark each end of last row to indicate end of front.

Cont in patt, work 2 rows more B, 2 E, 4 C, 2 D, 6 A, 4 E, 4 D, 2 E, 4 B, 4 A, 6 C, 4 D, 2 B, 6 E, 4 D, 4 A, 2 C, 2 B, 2 C, 4 D, 4 A, 4 B and 2 C.

Change to 3.25mm (no. 10) needles and D. K 3 rows. Cast off knitwise.

Making up

Press according to directions on ball band. With WS tog and matching stripes, fold up lower section of back at markers, then overlapping last 13 rows, fold down top section at markers. Join sides, taking all thicknesses into seams. Sew on buttons to correspond with buttonholes. Insert cushion pad and button to close.

Appliqué in Silk

○ The central panel of this beautiful silk cushion is decorated with a spray of applied flowers and details that are embroidered on afterwards.

Measurements

Cushion measures 45 x 30cm

Materials

HOW MUCH YARN

2 x 50g balls of Debbie Bliss Luxury Silk DK in each of colours
A – Duck Egg (shade 07) and
B – Ecru (shade 01)

1 skein in each of colours
C – Magenta (shade 04),
D – Lilac (shade 03) and
E – Lime (shade 09)

NEEDLES

Pair of 4mm (no. 8) needles

ADDITIONAL ITEMS

Tapestry needle
Cotton muslin backing fabric,
1 piece 45 x 30cm and 2 pieces
45 x 17cm
4 buttons
45 x 30cm cushion pad

Tension

24 sts and 32 rows measure 10cm square over st st on 4mm (no. 8) needles

IT IS ESSENTIAL TO WORK TO THE STATED TENSION TO ACHIEVE SUCCESS

Front

With 4mm (no. 8) needles and first ball of A, cast on 26 sts, then 52 sts in B and 26 sts with second ball of A. 104 sts. Beg with a k row, cont in st st and colours as set. Work 90 rows, twisting yarns tog on WS of work when changing colour to avoid holes forming. Cast off in colour.

Back

FIRST PIECE

With 4mm (no. 8) needles and A, cast on 26 sts, then 28 sts in B. 54 sts. Working in colours as set, cont as foll:

1st row: (RS) P1, (k1, p1) twice, k to end.

2nd row: P to last 5 sts, p1, (k1, p1) twice.

Rep these 2 rows throughout, working buttonholes on 18th, 36th, 54th and 72nd rows as foll:

Buttonhole row: (WS) P to last 5 sts, p1, k1, yo, k2tog, p1.

When 90 rows in all have been completed, cast off.

SECOND PIECE

With 4mm (no. 8) needles and B, cast on 28 sts, then 26 sts in A. 54 sts.

Working in colours as set, cont as foll:

1st row: (RS) K to last 5 sts, p1, (k1, p1) twice.

2nd row: P1, (k1, p1) twice, p to end.

Rep these 2 rows until 90 rows in all have been completed. Cast off.

Flower motifs

FLOWERS (Make 2 in C & 1 in D)
With 4mm (no. 8) needles and C, cast on 80 sts.

1st row: (RS) *K2, lift 1st of these sts over 2nd st and off right needle, rep from * to end. 40 sts.

2nd row: P to end.

3rd row: *K2tog, rep from * to end.

4th row: P to end.

5th–8th rows: Rep 3rd and 4th rows twice. 5 sts.

9th row: Lift 2nd, 3rd, 4th and 5th sts over 1st st.

Fasten off and join seam.

LEAVES (Make 2 in E)
With 4mm (no. 8) needles and E, cast on 5 sts.

1st row: (RS) K2, yo, k1, yo, k2.

2nd and foll alt rows: P to end.

3rd row: K3, yo, k1, yo, k3.

5th row: K4, yo, k1, yo, k4.

7th, 9th, 11th and 13th rows: Sl 1, k1, psso, k to last 2 sts, k2tog.

15th row: Sl 1, k2tog, psso.

Fasten off.

Making up

Block and press cushion pieces according to directions on yarn band.

Tack a piece of muslin fabric to WS of cushion front to provide stability. Tack muslin to cushion back pieces, turning under 1cm along one edge and slip stitching in place along edge of buttonhole band (leaving buttonholes exposed on first piece and taking folded edge almost to edge of button band on second piece.

Using the photograph as a guide, stitch the flowers and leaves in position on the cushion front. Embroider the flower centres in star stitch with straight stitch details, then work the stems in chain stitch using E and buds in French knots using C.

Lay the cushion front on a flat surface with RS up. Place first back piece on top, RS down, and matching colours. Lay the second back piece on top, RS down and matching colours again, so that button and buttonhole band overlap in the centre. Stitch together around outer edge, working through all layers of fabric. Turn RS out. Sew on buttons to correspond with buttonholes. Insert cushion pad and button cover closed.

Union Jack

○ Fly the flag with this stylish cushion – straight strips are appliquéd onto a stocking stitch background.

Measurements

Cushion measures 45 x 30cm

Materials

HOW MUCH YARN

3 x 50g balls of Rowan Wool Cotton in colour A – French Navy (shade 909)
1 ball in each of colours B – Antique (shade 900) and colour C – Rich (shade 911)

NEEDLES

Pair of 3.25mm (no. 10) needles
Pair of 4mm (no. 8) needles

ADDITIONAL ITEMS

30 x 45cm cushion pad
45cm zip fastener in navy blue
Navy, cream and red sewing threads and needle

Tension

22 sts and 30 rows, slightly stretched, measure 10cm square over st st on 3.25mm (no. 10) needles

IT IS ESSENTIAL TO WORK TO THE STATED TENSION TO ACHIEVE SUCCESS

Back

With 4mm (no. 8) needles and C, cast on 100 sts.

Change to 3.25mm (no. 10) needles.

Beg with a k row, cont in st st and stripe sequence of 2 rows C, 2 rows B, 6 rows A, 2 rows B, 2 rows C, 6 rows A (20 rows). Rep these 20 rows 3 times more. 80 rows in total.

Now work 2 rows C, 2 rows B, 6 rows A, 2 rows B and 2 rows C. 94 rows in total. Cast off using a 4mm (no. 8) needle.

Front

With 4mm (no. 8) needles and A, cast on 100 sts.

Change to 3.25mm (no. 10) needles.

Cont in st st, with reverse sts marking positions of horizontal and vertical appliqué stripes as foll:

1st row: (RS) K41, p1, k16, p1, k41.

2nd row: P41, k1, p16, k1, p41.

Rep these 2 rows 17 times more. 36 rows in total.

37th row: (RS) P42, k16, p42.

38th row: P to end.

39th row: K to end.

Rep 38th and 39th rows 9 times more. 57 rows in total.

58th row: (WS) K42, p16, k42.

Rep 1st and 2nd rows 18 times more. 94 rows in total. Cast off using a 4mm (no. 8) needle.

Cross

HORIZONTAL RED STRIPE

With 4mm (no. 8) needles and C, cast on 100 sts.

Change to 3.25mm (no. 10) needles.

Beg with a k row, work 12 rows in st st. Cast off using a 4mm (no. 8) needle.

Use short lengths of contrast yarn to place two markers on lower edge, 45 sts in from each side edge and 10 sts apart. Rep on upper edge.

VERTICAL RED STRIPE (make 2)

With 4mm (no. 8) needles and C, cast on 30 sts.

Change to 3.25mm (no. 10) needles.

Beg with a k row, work 12 rows in st st. Cast off using a 4mm (no. 8) needle.

Sew one side edge of one vertical stripe to 10 sts between markers on lower edge of horizontal stripe. Rep with other vertical stripe on top edge to form a red cross.

UPPER RIGHT WHITE BORDER

With 3.25mm (no. 10) needles, B and RS of red cross facing, beg at right of cast-off edge of horizontal stripe and pick up and k 45 sts from cast-off edge, 1 st at inner corner and 29 sts from edge of vertical stripe. 75 sts.

1st row: P27, p2tog, p1 (corner st), p2tog tbl, p43.

2nd row: K42, ssk, k1, k2tog, k26.

3rd row: P25, p2tog, p1, p2tog tbl, p41.

Cast off using a 4mm (no. 8) needle, dec as set.

LOWER LEFT WHITE BORDER

Turn cross through 180 degrees and, beg at right of cast-on edge of red horizontal stripe, work to match Upper right white border.

UPPER LEFT WHITE BORDER

With 3.25mm (no. 10) needles, B and RS of red cross facing, beg at left edge of upper red vertical stripe and pick up and k 29 sts from left edge of vertical stripe, 1 st at inner corner and 45 sts from top edge of horizontal stripe. 75 sts.

1st row: P43, p2tog, p1 (corner st), p2tog tbl, p27.

2nd row: K26, ssk, k1, k2tog, k42.

3rd row: P41, p2tog, p1, p2tog tbl, p25.

Cast off using a 4mm (no. 8) needle, dec as set.

LOWER RIGHT WHITE BORDER

Turn cross through 180 degrees and, beg at left of red vertical stripe, work to match Upper left white border.

Diagonals

UPPER RIGHT DIAGONAL STRIPE
With 4mm (no. 8) needles and B, cast on 42 sts.

1st row: (RS) K to last 2 sts, inc in next st, k1. 43 sts.

2nd row: Inc in first st, p to end. 44 sts.

Cut off B and join in C.

3rd row: Inc in first st, k to last 2 sts, inc in next st, k1. 46 sts.

4th row: Inc in first st, p to end. 47 sts.

5th row: Ssk, k to last 2 sts, inc in next st, k1. 47 sts.

6th row: Inc in first st, p to last 2 sts, p2tog tbl. 47 sts.

Cut off C and join in B.

7th row: Ssk, k to last 2 sts, k2tog. 45 sts.

8th row: P to last 2 sts, p2tog tbl. 44 sts.

9th–12th rows: Rep 7th and 8th rows twice more. 38 sts. Cast off.

LOWER LEFT DIAGONAL STRIPE
Work as given for Upper right diagonal stripe.

UPPER LEFT DIAGONAL STRIPE
With 4mm (no. 8) needles and B, cast on 42 sts.

1st row: (RS) Inc in first st, k to end. 43 sts.

2nd row: P to last 2 sts, inc in next st, p1. 44 sts.

3rd row: Inc in first st, k to last 2 sts, inc in next st, k1. 46 sts.

4th row: P to last 2 sts, inc in next st, p1. 47 sts.

5th row: Inc in first st, k to last 2 sts, k2tog. 47 sts.

6th row: P2tog, p to last 2 sts, inc in next st, p1. 47 sts.

Cut off B and join in C.

7th row: Ssk, k to last 2 sts, k2tog. 45 sts.

8th row: P2tog, p to end. 44 sts.

9th and 10th rows: As 7th and 8th rows. 41 sts.

Cut off C and join in B.

11th and 12 rows: As 7th and 8th rows. 38 sts. Cast off.

LOWER RIGHT DIAGONAL STRIPE
Work as given for Upper left diagonal stripe.

Making up

Press all pieces according to directions on ball band.

With cast-on edge at top, lay front flat and pin centre cross in place, so that edges of cross just cover all reverse sts on RS of front. Stitch in place, using B to backstitch through cast-off edges of all four quarters. Match stitch for stitch on horizontal edges, and fit evenly where vertical edges cover vertical lines of reverse sts.

Now sew diagonal stripes in place, using photo as a guide. Note position of broader white stripe on each diagonal.

Sew front to back on three sides, leaving cast-off edges open. Set zip into opening, sewing cast-off edges close to teeth of zip, and joining front and back for about 1.5cm to cover tapes at each end of zip. Insert cushion pad.

Raised Increasing (2)

Don't worry if you find the different kinds of increasing confusing, your pattern will tell you which type to use. The steps in this Knitting School and in the previous issue form a reference for decorative and invisible raised increasing.

Invisible raised increasing on a knit row

① Open the needles slightly and you will see a horizontal strand of yarn between the stitches on each needle. Insert the left-hand needle under this strand from front to back.

② Knit into the back of the strand. This twists the stitch, which is what makes it invisible in the final fabric.

③ Wrap the yarn around the right-hand needle and slide the stitch off the left-hand needle in the usual way.

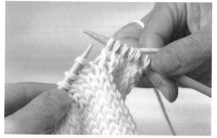

④ A stitch is created without a hole beneath it as there is in decorative raised increasing.

Increases are used to shape a garment by adding stitches in a row to make it larger. Raised increasing is done by picking up a horizontal strand between two stitches and working it as if it were a stitch. In the previous issue we looked at the decorative version and here we show how to make invisible raised increases.

Invisible raised increasing on a purl row

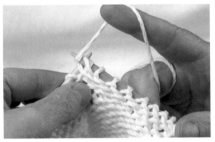

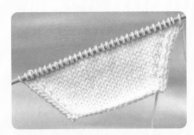

Invisible raised increasing increases the size of the knitted fabric. Twisting the stitch as you work it makes the increase nearly invisible. It can be worked at any point across the row. Here it is worked at both ends of the row creating small ridges.

1. Again, open the needles slightly and you will see a horizontal strand of yarn between the stitches on each needle. Insert the left-hand needle under this strand from front to back.

2. Purl into the back of the strand, which twists the stitch, and wrap the yarn around the needle in the usual way. Slide the stitch off the left-hand needle and you have created an extra stitch.

3. An extra stitch is made without creating a hole beneath it as you do in decorative raised increasing.

Folk Art Cushion

○ Traditional colours and embroidered motifs give this cushion a homely, folksy appeal.

Measurements

Cushion measures 38cm square

Materials

HOW MUCH YARN

3 x 100g balls of Rowan Pure Wool Aran in colour A – Ivory (shade 670)

1 ball in each of colours B – Burlesque (shade 689) and C – Vert (shade 686)

NEEDLES

Pair of 5.5mm (no. 5) needles

ADDITIONAL ITEMS

Blunt-ended wool needle

40cm square cushion pad

Tension

17 sts and 21 rows measure 10cm square over st st on 5.5mm (no. 5) needles

IT IS ESSENTIAL TO WORK TO THE STATED TENSION TO ACHIEVE SUCCESS

Note: Work motifs on Front in B using the intarsia technique with a separate small ball of yarn (or wind yarn on to bobbins) for each one. Twist yarns tog at edges of motifs when changing colours to prevent holes forming. When working motifs, strand or weave colour A across the WS of the work.

Front

With 5.5mm (no. 5) needles and A, cast on 65 sts. Beg with a k row, cont in st st and work 12 rows. Join in B. Cont in st st, work in patt from chart as foll:

1st row: (RS) K7 B, k across 30 sts of 1st row of chart reading from right to left, then rep 21 motif sts again reading from left to right, k7 B.

2nd row: P7 B, p across 21 motif sts of 2nd row of chart, reading from right to left, then p across 30 sts of 2nd row of chart reading from left to right, p7 B.

Cont in patt as set from chart until 61 rows have been completed. Cut off B. Cont in A, work 12 more rows, ending with a RS row. Cast off.

Back

TOP SECTION

With 5.5mm (no. 5) needles and A, cast on 65 sts. Beg with a k row, cont in st st until work measures 23cm from beg, ending with a p row. Work opening edge as foll:

Next row: (RS) K to end.

Next row: K1, (p1, k1) to end.

Next row: K to end.

Next row: P1, (k1, p1) to end.

Rep last 4 rows twice more. Cast off.

BOTTOM SECTION

Work as given for Top section until work measures 18cm from beg, ending with a p row. Work 2 rows as given for opening edge of Top section. Cast off.

Making up

Press according to directions on ball band. Using C, embroider chain stitch lines between motifs on front as shown in the picture. Keep the chain stitches fairly large and even. Work leaves (groups of three lazy daisy stitches) at intervals as shown.

Lay the cushion front with right side facing up. Place the top section then bottom section of back panels on top, with right sides facing down and overlapping opening edges in the centre. Join together by backstitching around outer edges. Turn right side out through back opening. Insert cushion pad.

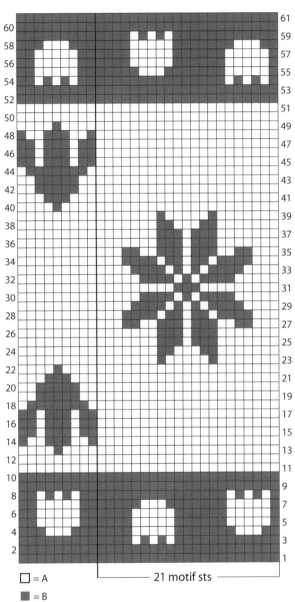

□ = A
■ = B

21 motif sts

Winter Wonder

○ With its knitted-in snowflakes and soft, natural colouring, this cushion with a cable-trimmed centre panel looks very Scandinavian.

Measurements

Cushion measures 45 x 45cm

Materials

HOW MUCH YARN

2 x 50g balls of Debbie Bliss Blue Faced Leicester DK in colour A – Stone (shade 05)

3 balls in colour B – Grey (shade 03)

1 ball in colour C – Gold (shade 06)

NEEDLES

Pair of 4mm (no. 8) needles

Cable needle

ADDITIONAL ITEMS

45cm square cushion pad

Tension

22 sts and 28 rows measure 10cm square over st st on 4mm (no. 8) needles

IT IS ESSENTIAL TO WORK TO THE STATED TENSION TO ACHIEVE SUCCESS

Front

CENTRE PANEL

With 4mm (no. 8) needles and A, cast on 77 sts.

1st row: (RS) K22, p1, k4, p1, k21, p1, k4, p1, k22.

2nd row: P22, k1, p4, k1, p21, k1, p4, k1, p22.

3rd row: K22, p1, C4F, p1, k21, p1, C4F, p1, k22.

4th row: As 2nd row.

These 4 rows set st st and cable patt. Place Chart 1 as foll:

*Next row: (RS) K1, k across next 21 sts as 1st row of Chart 1, p1, k4, p1, k21, p1, k4, p1, k across next 21 sts as 1st row of Chart 1, k1.

Cont in patt as now set, keeping cable patt correct and working from Chart 1 until all 28 rows have been completed.*

Next row: (RS) K22, p1, k4, p1, k across next 21 sts as 1st row of Chart 1, p1, k4, p1, k22.

Cont in patt as set until 28 rows from Chart 1 have been completed. Now rep from * to *. Patt 4 rows. Cast off.

BORDER

With 4mm (no. 8) needles, B and RS of work facing, pick up and k 73 sts along one outer edge of centre panel. Beg with a k row, cont in st st and patt from Chart 2, AT SAME TIME inc 1 st at each end of 2nd and every foll row until there are 97 sts. Work 1 row straight (14th row of Chart is complete). Cast off.

Work border in same way on rem 3 outer edges of centre panel.

Back

With 4mm (no. 8) needles and B, cast on 97 sts. Cont in spot patt as foll, stranding or weaving yarn not in use loosely across WS of work:

1st–4th rows: With B and beg with a k row, work 4 rows in st st.

5th row: *K3 B, 1 C, 2 B, rep from * to last st, 1 B.

6th–10th rows: With B and beg with a p row, work 5 rows in st st.

11th row: K6 B, *1 C, 5 B, rep from * to last st, 1 B.

12th row: With B, p to end.

These 12 rows form patt. Rep them until Back measures approximately 45cm from beg, ending with 4 rows in B. Cast off.

Making up

Join front borders along diagonal edges. With C and using photograph as a guide, embroider 5 evenly spaced stars into plain areas between each snowflake. Each star is made up of 4 straight sts with a small diagonal st in centre to hold long threads in place.

With RS facing, sew front and back together around three sides. Turn right side out, insert cushion pad and use mattress st to close open edge.

Chart 1

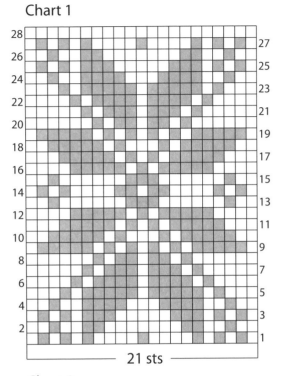

□ = A
▨ = B
▨ = C

21 sts

Chart 2

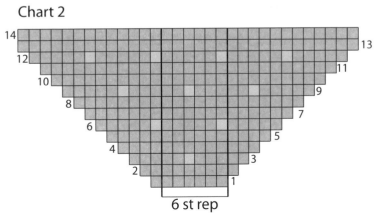

6 st rep

Your Chunky Throw

○ It's all happening in this square - moss stitch inside a cable diamond with bobbles at either end. Enjoy the challenge!

Moss Stitch Diamond Square

Moss Stitch Diamond Square

Measurements

Finished square is 20 x 20cm

Materials

Ball of cream yarn provided (save any leftover yarn)

Pair of 10mm (no.000) needles provided

Cable needle

Tension

9.5 sts and 12 rows measure 10cm square over patt.

IT IS ESSENTIAL TO WORK TO THE STATED
TENSION TO ACHIEVE SUCCESS

What to do

With 10mm (no. 000) needles and cream yarn, cast on 19 sts.

K 2 rows.

1st row: K2, p15, k2.

2nd row: K6, p1, (k1, p1) 3 times, k6.

3rd row: K2, p3, (Tw2R) twice, MB, (Tw2L) twice, p3, k2.

4th row: K5, (p1, k1) 4 times, p1, k5.

5th row: K2, p2, (Tw2R) twice, k1, p1, k1, (Tw2L) twice, p2, k2.

6th row: K4, (p1, k1) 5 times, p1, k4.

7th row: K2, p1, (Tw2R) twice, k1, (p1, k1) twice, (Tw2L) twice, p1, k2.

8th row: K3, (p1, k1), 6 times, p1, k3.

9th row: K2, (Tw2R) twice, k1, (p1, k1) 3 times, (Tw2L) twice, k2.

10th row: K2, (p1, k1) 7 times, p1, k2.

11th row: K2, (Tw2L) twice, p1, (k1, p1) 3 times, (Tw2R) twice, k2.

12th row: As 8th row.

13th row: K2, p1, (Tw2L) twice, p1, (k1, p1) twice, (Tw2R) twice, p1, k2.

14th row: As 6th row.

15th row: K2, p2, (Tw2L) twice, p1, k1, p1, (Tw2R) twice, p2, k2.

16th row: As 4th row.

17th row: K2, p3, (Tw2L) twice, MB, (Tw2R) twice, p3, k2.

K 3 rows.

Cast off purlwise.